How to use this book

This Reception Handwriting workbook is matched to the Early Years Foundation Stage Framework and is designed to improve early handwriting skills.

Handy **tips** are included throughout.

Activities split into three levels of difficulty – **Challenge 1**, **Challenge 2** and **Challenge 3** – to help progression.

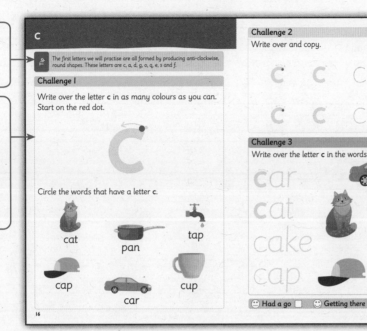

Opportunities for **self-evaluation** are included throughout.

Starter check recaps skills already learned.

Four **Progress checks** included throughout the book for ongoing assessment and monitoring progress.

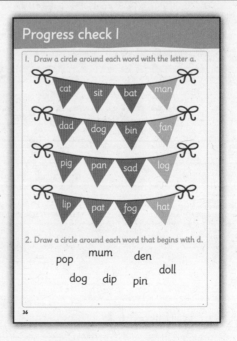

Contents

ACKNOWLEDGEMENTS

Published by Collins
An imprint of HarperCollins*Publishers* Ltd
1 London Bridge Street
London SE1 9GF

HarperCollins*Publishers*
Macken House
39/40 Mayor Street Upper
Dublin 1
D01 C9W8
Ireland

ISBN 978-0-00-853463-9

First published 2023

10 9 8 7 6 5 4 3 2 1

All rights reserved. No part of this
publication may be reproduced, stored
in a retrieval system, or transmitted, in
any form or by any means, electronic,
mechanical, photocopying, recording or
otherwise, without the prior permission
of Collins.

British Library Cataloguing in
Publication Data.
A CIP record of this book is available
from the British Library.

Publishers: Fiona McGlade and
Jennifer Hall
Author: Shelley Welsh
Series Editor: Dr Jane Medwell
Project Management and Editorial:
Chantal Addy

Cover Design: Sarah Duxbury
Inside Concept Design: Ian Wrigley
Typesetting and Artwork: Jouve India
Private Limited
Production: Emma Wood
Printed in India by Multivista Global Pvt. Ltd

MIX
Paper | Supporting
responsible forestry
FSC™ C007454

This book is produced from independently
certified FSC™ paper to ensure responsible
forest management.

For more information visit:
www.harpercollins.co.uk/green

Guidance for parents

Handwriting at home — the Reception year

Parental support can make a huge difference to a child's confidence and achievements when they first start to learn handwriting. Basic handwriting skills are a great basis for more complex literacy skills later; a child who can write letters automatically can attend to all those other tricky aspects of writing — getting ideas, putting them in order, spelling, etc.

There are three very clear priorities for your child in relation to handwriting in Reception:
- motivation and enjoyment
- holding a writing tool
- making the correct letter formations.

Motivation and enjoyment

Early learning happens when children enjoy the experience. As well as using this workbook, all sorts of manipulative activities are good preparation for handwriting. Encourage your child to:
- colour (and scribble) with crayons, chalks, pens, paintbrushes and pencils
- write 'messages' to you (which they will need to read out)
- take part in playdough and clay activities to flex developing hand muscles
- thread, cut and arrange small objects, construction kits, etc.

The early pages of this workbook focus on learning to draw lines, crosses and circles to help develop pencil control. As you work through the book, point out improvements in your child's pencil control, so that they can take pride in getting better at handwriting.

Holding a writing tool

A young child's pencil grip will gradually develop from a simple palmar grip (a fist) to the point where they can hold the pencil in three or four fingers and, eventually, hold the pencil between the thumb and index finger with the pencil supported on the middle finger.

Show your child how you hold a pencil and help them to get better at it gradually. Aim for your child to have control of the writing tool but not to grip it too hard, as this will tire their hands and arms. Most young children do best with thicker, triangular pencils/pens or crayons, if you have them. However, a whole range of tools (crayons, felt-tips, etc) is useful.

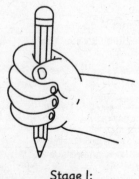

Stage 1:
palmar

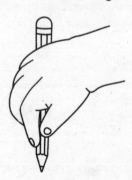

Stage 2:
all fingers

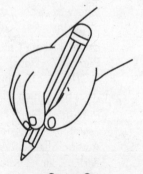

Stage 3:
three–four fingers

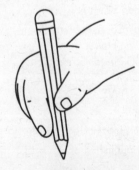

Stage 4:
supported on middle finger

Left-handed children

Your child might have developed a "hand preference" for their left or right hand already, but many children will still be using both hands at different times. Although most children are right-handed, around 10 percent of any population is left-handed, so notice which hand your child prefers to use. Young children do forget, so once you know which hand they prefer, you might need to remind them when they start an activity.

Left-handed children may like to sit on slightly higher chairs and hold the pencil slightly further from the point to cope with the demands of letters designed for right-handers.

Letter formation

The most important priority in your child's early handwriting endeavours is to form each letter correctly, starting at the right point. Children who can do this will be able to write letters effortlessly and join them up in due course. If your child tries to start letters in the wrong place, gently redirect them to the correct starting point for the letter.

This workbook uses letter formations which are easy for children to do correctly and leads effortlessly into joined writing in Years 1 and 2. On pages 6 and 7, you will see all the letters with arrows to show how they are formed and where each letter starts. The most important priority is for your child to learn each letter as a movement (not just a picture).

At this point in learning handwriting, do not worry about the size and evenness of letters, but do try to get the movement right.

Practising handwriting with your child

With practice, young children quickly learn to "feel" the correct letter movement and get it right every time. We recommend doing frequent short practice sessions of 5–10 minutes in Reception. Though this does not sound like very much, a few minutes a day really can make a positive difference.

When your child uses this workbook for handwriting practice, they will probably slant the page. Left-handers usually slant the top of the page to the right and right-handers slant the top of the page to the left. This is good practice. If your child can sit at a table to write, it will help them get used to doing this.

We recommend using a pencil for handwriting practice, because a plain lead pencil has a good combination of grip and slip. But if your child prefers crayons or pens, why not?

Self-evaluation

Talking with your child about their handwriting practice is very helpful. The "evaluation strips" at the end of every double page in this workbook allow your child to estimate their own progress.

The "self-evaluation grids" in the "progress checks" are designed to help you discuss your child's progress at handwriting.

The "progress chart" on the last page allows your child to record how they feel about their handwriting after completing the workbook. It is always good to notice and praise efforts or improvements as it helps your child become confident and proud of their handwriting.

Letter formations

Lower-case letter formations

a b c d e

f g h i j k

l m n o p

q r s t u

v w x y z

6 Lower-case letter formations

Capital letter formations

A B C D E

F G H I J K

L M N O P

Q R S T U

V W X Y Z

7

Holding a pencil

Tip

Pick up your pencil. Which hand do you prefer?

Left or right ?

Ask an adult to help you hold your pencil using your fingers and thumb.
Practise picking up your pencil and holding it properly.

Trace the line with your finger. Start on the red dot.

Join the dots with your pencil. Start on the red dot.

Now draw your own wavy line. Start on the red dot and follow the arrow.

Challenge 2

Draw a line from the red dot to help the mouse get home.

Challenge 3

Draw a line from the red dots to draw the strings for the kites.

Holding a pencil

Challenge 1

Join the dots to finish the igloo.

Start at the red dots and join the dots to complete the patterns on the hat. Then colour in the patterns.

Challenge 2

Start on the red dot and follow the arrow to make six circles.

Challenge 3

Draw a circle around the things you would find in a kitchen.

Holding a pencil

Follow the arrows to join the dots. Start on the red dot.

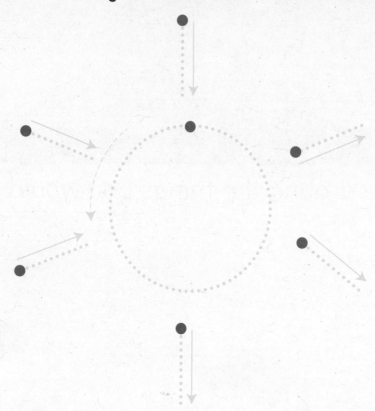

Draw circles around the animals in the picture below.

Challenge 2

Join the dots to complete the lines. Start on the red dot.

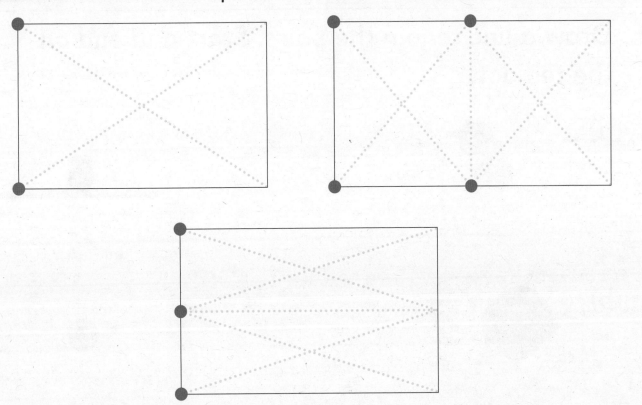

Challenge 3

Draw a cross like this ✕ over each letter in your name.

a   b   c   d   e   f   g

h   i   j   k   l   m   n

o   p   q   r   s   t   u

v   w   x   y   z

Starter check

1. Draw a line to join the pairs. Start and end on the red dot.

a)

b)

c)

d)

2. Draw your own zigzag line under the one below. Start on the red dot.

3. Draw a line to help the dog find the bone on the other side of the maze. Try not to touch the sides!

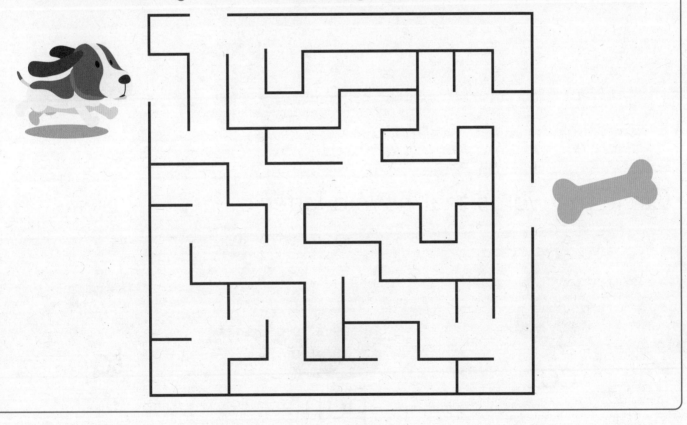

	Not sure	Working on it	Yes I can
I can draw a line from left to right			
I can draw circles			
I can draw crosses			

Tip The first letters we will practise are all formed by producing anti-clockwise, round shapes. These letters are c, a, d, g, o, q, e, s and f.

Challenge 1

Write over the letter **c** in as many colours as you can. Start on the red dot.

Circle the words that have a letter **c**.

cat

pan

tap

cap

car

cup

Challenge 2

Write over and copy.

c c c c c

c c c c c

Challenge 3

Write over the letter **c** in the words.

car

cat

cake

cap

Challenge 1

Write over the letter **a** in as many colours as you can.
Start on the red dot.

Circle the words that have a letter **a**.

rat

pin

hat

tap

bag

dog

Challenge 2

Write over and copy.

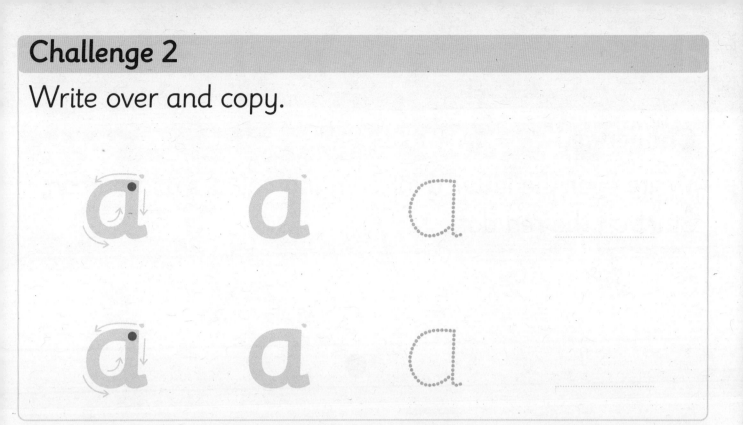

a   a   a

a   a   a

Challenge 3

Write over the letter **a** in the words.

ant

apple

axe

arm

d

Write over the letter **d** in as many colours as you can. Start on the red dot.

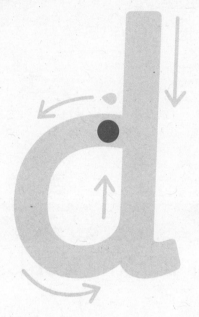

Circle the words that have a letter **d**.

dog

cat

dig

pen

bed

doll

Challenge 2

Write over and copy.

Challenge 3

Write over the letter **d** in the words.

dog

doll

dig

bed

g

Challenge 1

Write over the letter **g** in as many colours as you can. Start on the red dot.

Circle the words that have a letter **g**.

log

ten

wag

dog

bed

dig

22

Challenge 2

Write over and copy.

Challenge 3

Write over the letter **g** in the words.

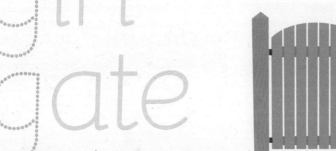

bag

dog

girl

gate

Challenge 1

Write over the letter **o** in as many colours as you can. Start on the red dot.

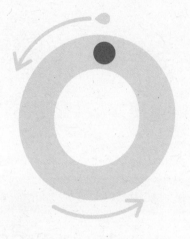

Circle the words that have a letter **o**.

log

six

wag

dog

hop

rod

Challenge 2

Write over and copy.

Challenge 3

Write over the letter **o** in the words.

dog   log

on   hop

fog   one

Challenge 1

Write over the letter **q** in as many colours as you can. Start on the red dot.

Circle all the letters that are **q**.

o

c

q

a

d

q

g

c

q

Challenge 2

Write over and copy.

q   q   q   q

q   q   q   q

Challenge 3

Write over the letter **q** in the words.

queen

quiet

quilt

queue

Challenge 1

Write over the letter **e** in as many colours as you can. Start on the red dot.

Circle the words that have a letter **e**.

red

car

ten

bed

pot

net

Challenge 2

Write over and copy.

Challenge 3

Write over the letter **e** in the words.

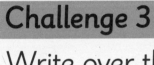

bed

net

leg

red

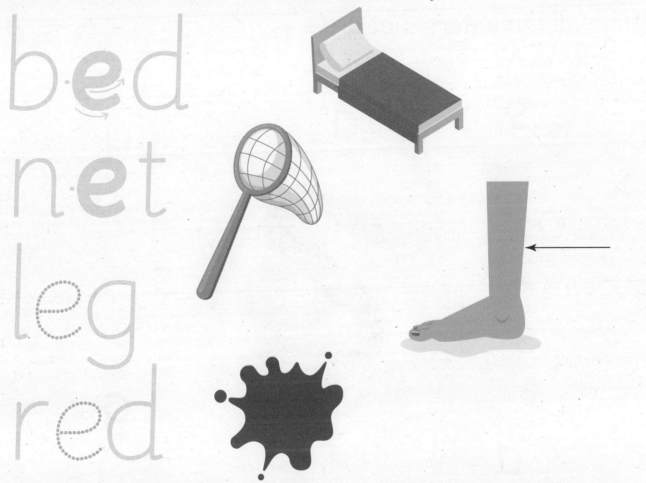

Challenge I

Write over the letter **s** in as many colours as you can. Start on the red dot.

Circle all the letters that are **s**.

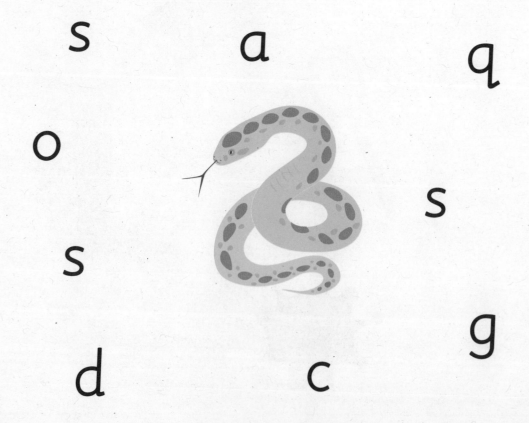

s   a   q

o

                                        s

s

                              g

    d   c

Challenge 2

Write over and copy.

s s s

s s s

Challenge 3

Write over the letter **s** in the words.

sad   sock

sum   sea

mess   fuss

kiss   pass

f

Challenge 1

Write over the letter **f** in as many colours as you can. Start on the red dot.

Circle all the letters that are **f**.

o f a q

o

f s

d c f g

Challenge 2

Write over and copy.

Challenge 3

Write over the letter **f** in the words.

fan   fun

fish   fly

puff   stuff

cuff   fluff

c, a, d, g, o, q, e, s and f

Challenge 1

Write over the letters.

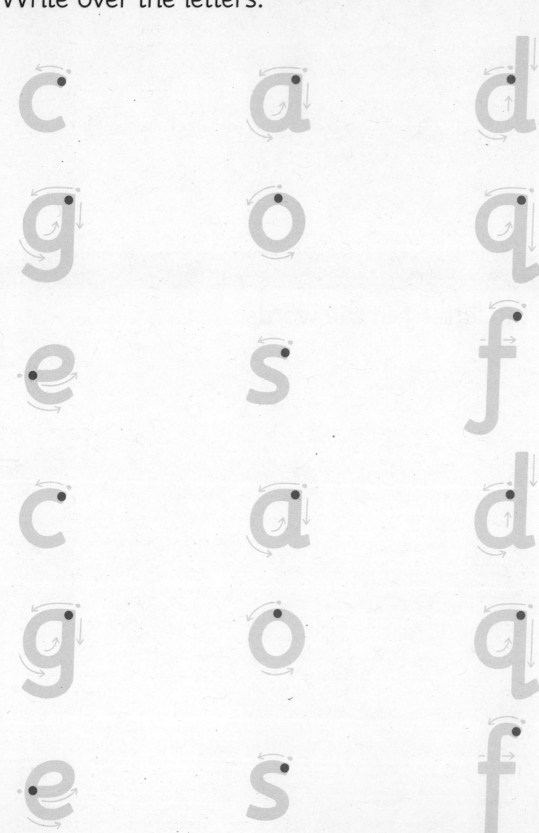

Challenge 2

Write over the dotted letters at the beginning of each word.

cat

dog

sun

cap

Challenge 3

Add the missing letters to the middle of each of these words.

a o e

c_t

d_g

n_t

b_g

Progress check 1

1. Draw a circle around each word with the letter a.

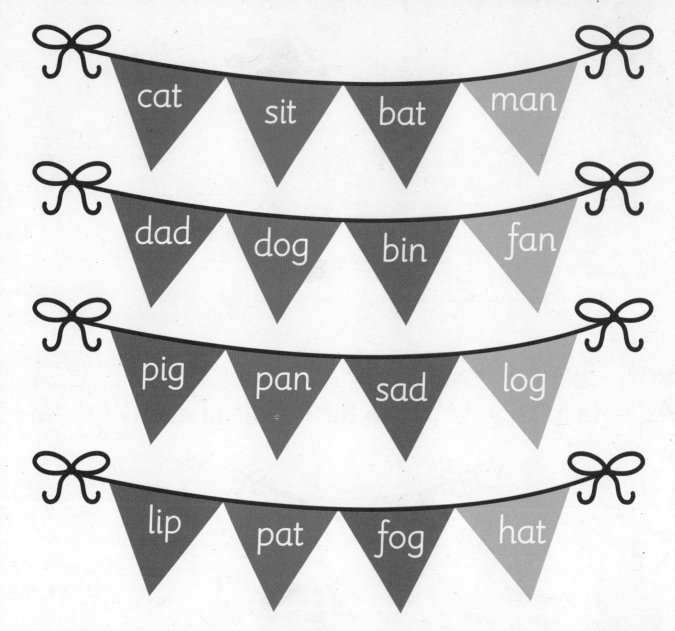

cat   sit   bat   man

dad   dog   bin   fan

pig   pan   sad   log

lip   pat   fog   hat

2. Draw a circle around each word that begins with d.

mum   den

pop   doll

dog   dip   pin

3. Draw a line to each word that starts with the letters on the left. One has been done for you. Start on the red dot.

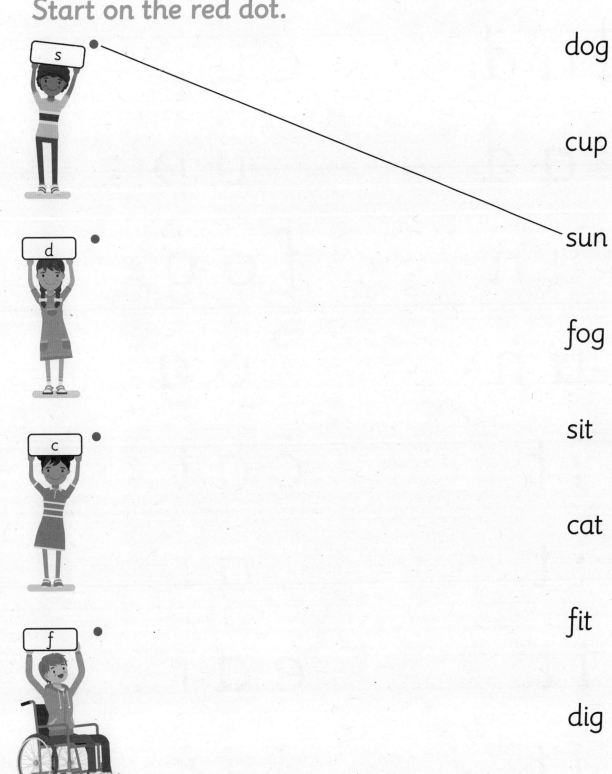

dog

cup

sun

fog

sit

cat

fit

dig

4. Write over the dotted letters to copy those that are in red at the start of each word.

dad	cup
dad	cup
sun	fog
sun	fog
sit	cat
sit	cat
fit	ear
fit	ear

5. Write over each of the following letters, then write your own letters on the lines.

g g g ___ ___ ___

q q q ___ ___ ___

o o o ___ ___ ___

e e e ___ ___ ___

s s s ___ ___ ___

f f f ___ ___ ___

	☺ Not sure	☺ Working on it	☺ Yes I can
I can write round letters (c, a, o)			
I can write letters that go up and down (d, f, g, q)			
I can write tricky letters (e, s)			

i

Tip

The next set of letters we will practise are all formed by going down and off in a different direction. These letters are i, l, t, u, y, j and k.

Challenge 1

Write over the letter **i** in as many colours as you can. Start on the red dot.

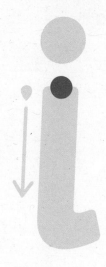

Circle all the letters that are **i**.

40

Challenge 2

Write over and copy.

i i i

i i i

Challenge 3

Write over the letter **i** in the words.

ink   in   dip

sip   bin   sick

lid   lip   him

Challenge 1

Write over the letter **l** in as many colours as you can. Start on the red dot.

Circle all the words that have a letter **l**.

lolly

lips

dig

lit

leg

doll

Challenge 2

Write over and copy.

l l l l

l l l l

Challenge 3

Write over the letter **l** in the words.

lid   lip   lap

lot   leg   lick

fell   well   tell

t

Challenge 1

Write over the letter **t** in as many colours as you can. Start on the red dot.

Circle all the words that have a letter **t**.

tap   tall

dot   hat

pin   cat

44

Challenge 2

Write over and copy.

t t t

t t t

Challenge 3

Write over the letter **t** in the words.

tap tag tan

hat bat hot

sit but fat

😐 Had a go ☐   🙂 Getting there ☐   😃 Got it! ☐

Challenge 1

Write over the letter **u** in as many colours as you can. Start on the red dot.

Circle all the letters that are **u**.

Challenge 2

Write over and copy.

u u u

u u u

Challenge 3

Write over the letter **u** in the words.

sun mud mum

sum dug fun

luck but suck

y

Write over the letter **y** in as many colours as you can. Start on the red dot.

Circle all the letters that are **y**.

y   u

u   u

y   y

Challenge 2

Write over and copy.

Challenge 3

Write over the letter **y** in the words.

yes   yap   yell

pay   daddy   say

away mummy lay

Challenge 1

Write over the letter **j** in as many colours as you can. Start on the red dot.

Circle all the letters that are **j**.

Challenge 2

Write over and copy.

j j j _____

j j j _____

Challenge 3

Write over the letter **j** in the words.

jam jar jug

jog jab jump

just jelly juggle

k

Write over the letter **k** in as many colours as you can. Start on the red dot.

Circle all the letters that are **k**.

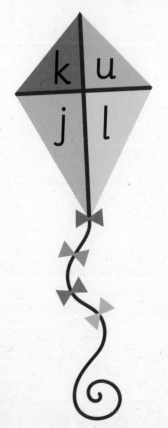

Challenge 2

Write over and copy.

k   k   k

k   k   k

Challenge 3

Write over the letter **k** in the words.

kite   kick   kit

key   kind   kiwi

keep   kid   koala

i, l, t, u, y, j and k

Challenge 1

Circle the letters i, l, t, u, y, j and k in the alphabet.

Write over the letters.

i l t u y j k

Challenge 2

 To complete the challenge, write the words from the grid below on individual cards to show your child.

Draw a cross on each word when you see it on the card.

jig	tail	cut
tug	kick	sky
lick	jog	yet

Challenge 3

Write over the letters in the words below.

jug   jug

lay   lay

kettle   kettle

still   still

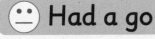 Had a go ☐   Getting there ☐   Got it! ☐

1. Draw a line to help the kitten find her mother.

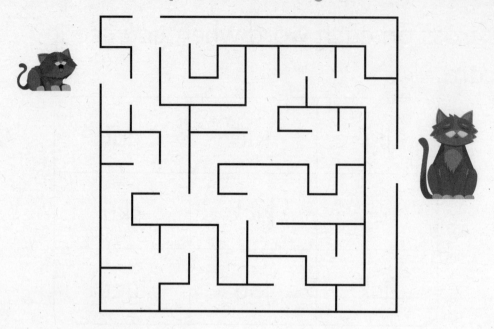

2. Write over and copy.

3. Write over and copy.

4. Make the letter **s** by drawing inside each snake.
   Start on the red dot.

5. Write over and copy.

6. Draw a circle around the words that have a letter **a**.

mat   dog   fit   pat

fat   tin   tap   net

7. Draw a circle around the words that have a letter **g**.

gap   lit   cup   get

sag   lay   tag   dig

8. Draw a circle around each letter u.

9. Join the dots.

10. Write over the grey letters.

I love jelly and ice cream.

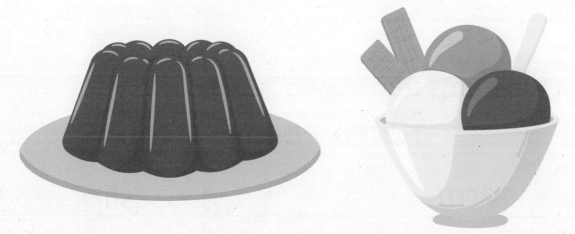

	😐 Not sure	🙂 Working on it	😃 Yes I can
I can write short letters (i, u)			
I can write letters that go up and down (l, y, j)			
I can write tricky letters (k, t)			

r

Tip The next set of letters we will practise are all formed by going down then going back upwards and over to the side. These letters are r, n, m, h, b and p.

Challenge 1

Write over the letter **r** in as many colours as you can. Start on the red dot.

Circle the words that have a letter **r**.

run   bear   tap

farm   slip

bar   bun

spin   drip

fur   pan   rabbit

Challenge 2

Write over and copy.

 r r r

r r r r

Challenge 3

Write over the letter **r** in the words.

red   car   far   rag

rat   run   tar   her

start   drag   card   tray

n

Write over the letter **n** in as many colours as you can. Start on the red dot.

Circle the words that have a letter **n**.

run

bean

rap

nod

nest

lip

bun

pan

far

fun

ban

pin

Challenge 2

Write over and copy.

n   n   n

n   n   n

Challenge 3

Write over the letters then copy the words onto the line below each.

on   den   fun

_____   _____   _____

sun   can   ant

_____   _____   _____

and   land   sand

_____   _____   _____

 Had a go ☐   Getting there ☐   Got it! ☐

m

Challenge 1

Write over the letter **m** in as many colours as you can. Start on the red dot.

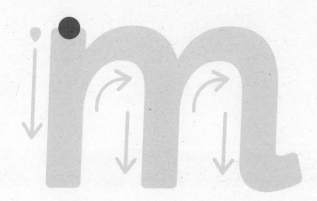

Circle the words that have a letter **m**.

nap

mum

pram

man

plan

nan

mad

nod

slam

map

can

far

64

Challenge 2

Write over and copy.

m   m   m   _____

m   m   m   _____

Challenge 3

Write over the letters then copy the words onto the
line below each.

man   ram   gum

_____   _____   _____

sum   jam   tummy

_____   _____   _____

farm   alarm   mummy

_____   _____   _____

h

Write over the letter **h** in as many colours as you can. Start on the red dot.

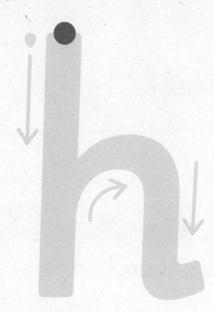

Circle the words that have a letter **h**.

him

pan

ham

hot

nap

hip

hop

sun

nip

hit

hum

her

Challenge 2

Write over and copy.

h h h

h h h

Challenge 3

Write over the letters then copy the words onto the line below each.

hot   hip   hut

hen   hat   hug

holly   hand   harm

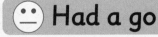

b

Write over the letter **b** in as many colours as you can. Start on the red dot.

Circle the words that have a letter **b**.

him

ban

bar

nap

hot

rabbit

hob

bun

nip

bit

dab

bubble

Challenge 2

Write over and copy.

b b b

b b b

Challenge 3

Write over the letters then copy the words onto the line below each.

big   boy   bug

band   crab   grab

baby   rabbit   bubble

Challenge 1

Write over the letter **p** in as many colours as you can.
Start on the red dot.

Circle the words that have a letter **p**.

gym   puppy

hum   bit

pan   bun

pat   dig

pop   put

nap

bit

Challenge 2

Write over and copy.

p   p   p

p   p   p

Challenge 3

Write over the letters then copy the words onto the line below each.

pat   pit   put

....

pet   cap   mop

....

popping   dripping

....

r, n, m, h, b and p

Write over and copy.

r   r   r

n   n   n

m   m   m

h   h   h

b   b   b

p   p   p

Challenge 2

Fill in the gaps using the letters below.

r   b   n

___un   ___all   ___et

Challenge 3

Fill in the gaps.

d p   ___ri___

d m   ___ru___

m k   ___on___ey

1. Write over and copy.

i   i   i

2. Write over and copy.

l   l   l

3. Write over and copy.

t   t   t

4. Write over and copy.

u   u   u

5. Write over and copy.

y   y   y

6. Write over and copy.

j   j   j

7. Write over and copy.

k   k   k

8. Write over and copy.

r   r   r   _____

9. Write over and copy.

n   n   n   _____

10. Write over and copy.

m   m   m   _____

11. Write over and copy.

h   h   h   _____

12. Write over and copy.

b   b   b   _____

13. Write over and copy.

p   p   p   _____

14. Write over and copy.

lit   lit   lit   lit

....

rub   rub   rub   rub

....

yell   yell   yell   yell

....

jump   jump   jump   jump

....

puppy   puppy   puppy   puppy

....

15. Write the letters in the spaces.

a   j......m   j......m   j......m

i   d......p   d......p   d......p

u   j......mp   j......mp   j......mp

d   pu......ing   pu......ing

	😐 Not sure	🙂 Working on it	😄 Yes I can
I can write short letters (r, n, m)			
I can write letters that go up and down (h, b, p)			
I can write letters in spaces			

77

v

The last set of letters we will practise are all formed by using straight, sharp lines and turns. These letters are v, w, x and z.

Challenge I

Write over the letter **v** in as many colours as you can. Start on the red dot.

Circle all the letters that are **v**.

m n v w n

i v

v

y

x a

z w v

c v k

Challenge 2

Write over and copy.

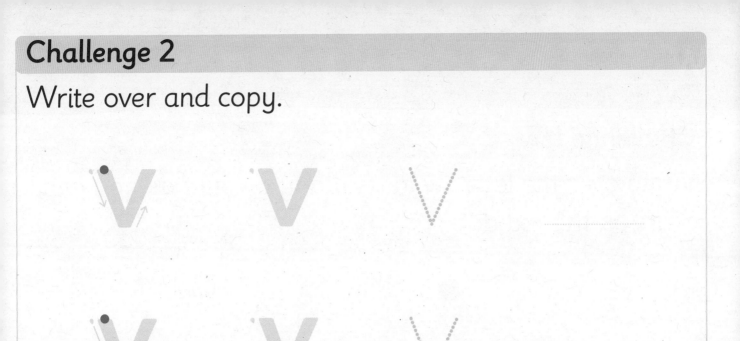

Challenge 3

Write over the letter **v** in the words.

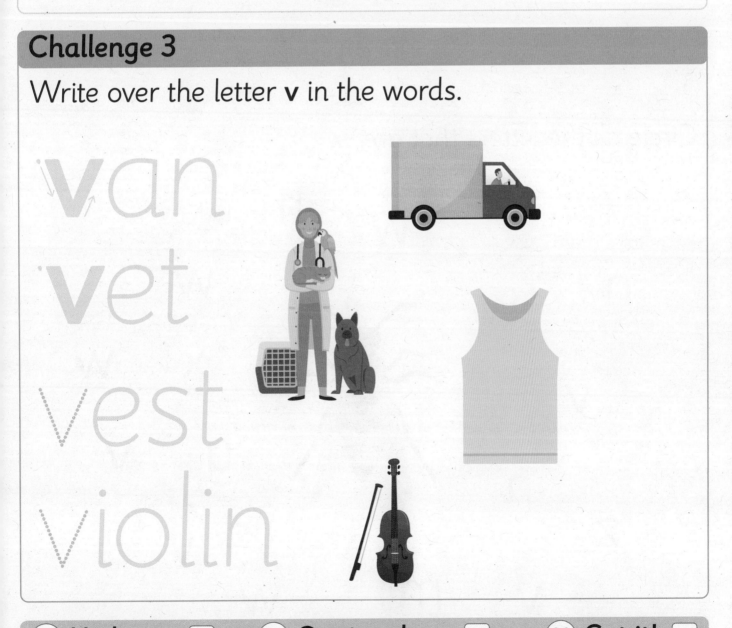

van

vet

vest

violin

Challenge 1

Write over the letter **w** in as many colours as you can. Start on the red dot.

Circle all the letters that are **w**.

Challenge 2

Write over and copy.

w   w   w   ....

w   w   w   ....

Challenge 3

Write over the letter **w** in the words.

wall   wag

win   wig

wall   wasp

Challenge 1

Write over the letter **x** in as many colours as you can. Start on the red dot.

Circle all the letters that are **x**.

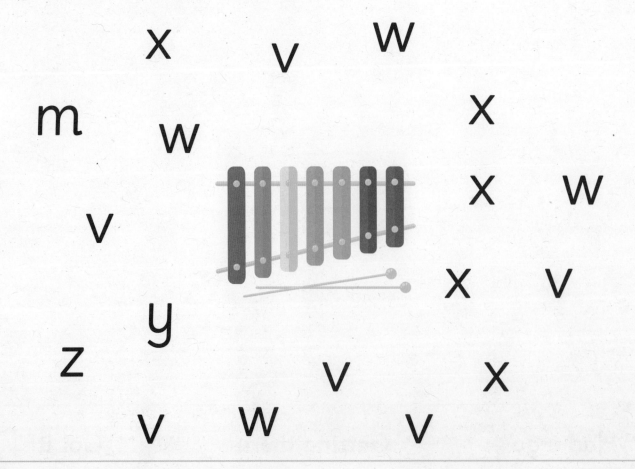

x   v   w

m   w   x

v   x w

y   x v

z   v   x

v   w   v

Challenge 2

Write over and copy.

Challenge 3

Write over the letter **x** in the words.

a**x**e

box

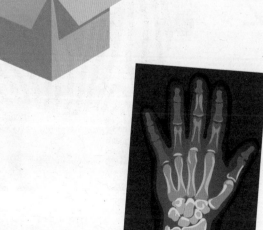

x-ray

Challenge 1

Write over the letter **z** in as many colours as you can.
Start on the red dot.

Circle all the letters that are **z**.

Challenge 2

Write over and copy.

z   z   z   z   _____

z   z   z   z   _____

Challenge 3

Write over the letter **z** in the words.

zig   zag

zebra   fizz

zoom   fuzzy

v, w, x and z

Circle the letters **v**, **w**, **x** and **z**.

a
x
c
d
v
p
y
w
z
o
f

Write over and copy the letters.

Challenge 2

Write over the dotted letters in the words.

van   wasp

tax   zoo

Challenge 3

Write the letters in the spaces.

 bu_____   bu_____   bu_____

 wa___e   wa___e   wa___e

 fi_____   fi_____   fi_____

 dra_____   dra_____   dra_____

Writing words

Write over and copy.

and   and

_____   _____

but   but

_____   _____

Challenge 2

Fill in the gaps.

a d   nd

b t   ut

Challenge 3

Fill in the gaps.

I like jelly ....
ice cream.

Mum likes jelly ....
she doesn't like ice cream.

Writing words

Write over and copy.

an   is   on

....

an   is   on

....

an   is   on

....

Challenge 2

Write over the letters.

There is an apple on the table.

Challenge 3

Fill in the gaps.

There _____ _____

apple _____ the table.

Progress check 4

1. Write over and copy.

a   b   c   d   e

f   g   h   i   j

k   l   m   n   o

p   q   r   s   t

u   v   w   x   y   z

2. Write the missing letters in each word below.

____an   ____an   ____an

____in   ____in   ____in

fo____   fo____   fo____

____ebra   ____ebra   ____ebra

3. Copy each word.

car	pat	fat

nip	sit	dip

pet	net	ten

bun	cut	run

4. Copy the words below.

Hickory dickory dock

The mouse ran up the clock

5. Write your name on the line below.

	☺ Not sure	☺ Working on it	☺ Yes I can
I can write w, v, x, z			
I can write over and copy words			
I can write letters in spaces			

Progress chart

Write over the ticks in the boxes to show how you feel about your handwriting.

	Not sure	Working on it	Yes I can!
I can write round letters (c, a, o)	✓	✓	✓
I can write letters that go up and down (d, f, g, q)	✓	✓	✓
I can write tricky letters (e, s)	✓	✓	✓
I can write short letters (i, u)	✓	✓	✓
I can write letters that go up and down (l, y, j)	✓	✓	✓
I can write tricky letters (k, t)	✓	✓	✓
I can write short letters (r, n, m)	✓	✓	✓
I can write letters that go up and down (h, b, p)	✓	✓	✓
I can write letters in spaces	✓	✓	✓
I can write w, v, x, z	✓	✓	✓
I can write over and copy words	✓	✓	✓